Liberia:

Malaria Operational Plan FY 2014

TABLE OF CONTENTS

EXECUTIVE SUMMARY

Malaria prevention and control is a major foreign assistance objective of the U.S. Government (USG). In May 2009, President Barack Obama announced the Global Health Initiative (GHI), a comprehensive effort to reduce the burden of disease and promote healthy communities and families around the world. The President's Malaria Initiative (PMI) is a core component of the GHI, along with HIV/AIDS, tuberculosis, maternal and child health, family planning and reproductive health, nutrition and neglected tropical diseases.

PMI was launched in June 2005 as a 5-year, $1.2 billion initiative to rapidly scale up malaria prevention and treatment interventions and reduce malaria-related mortality by 50% in 15 high-burden countries in sub-Saharan Africa. With passage of the 2008 Lantos-Hyde Act, funding for PMI was extended and the PMI strategy was revised to achieve Africa-wide impact by halving the burden of malaria in 70 percent of at-risk populations in sub-Saharan Africa. Programming of PMI activities follows the core principles of GHI: encouraging country ownership and investing in country-led plans and health systems; increasing impact and efficiency through strategic coordination and programmatic integration; strengthening and leveraging key partnerships, multilateral organizations, and private contributions; implementing a woman- and girl-centered approach; improving monitoring and evaluation (M&E); and promoting research and innovation.

Liberia began PMI-supported activities in FY 2008. Liberia's health infrastructure was severely damaged during the long civil war, which ended in 2003, leaving only about 45% of the population with access to essential health services. The entire population of approximately 3.8 million is at risk for malaria[1]. The 2011 Malaria Indicator Survey (MIS) showed malaria prevalence by microscopy at 28%. The National Malaria Control Program (NMCP) has produced a National Malaria Control Strategy for the years 2010-2015.

Liberia has received malaria funding from the Global Fund to Fight Aids, Tuberculosis and Malaria (Global Fund) since 2004. Currently, Liberia receives Global Fund support through a consolidated grant made up of Phase 2 of a Round 7, $37 million grant and Phase 1 of a Round 10, $60 million grant. With Phase 1 of the consolidated grant ending in 2013, Liberia is in the process of completing an assessment of Phase 1 and an application for Phase 2 renewal.

Based on progress and experiences over six years of PMI implementation, this FY 2014 Malaria Operational Plan (MOP) for Liberia was drafted during a planning exercise carried out in April 2013 by representatives from the United States Agency for International Development (USAID) and the Centers for Disease Control and Prevention (CDC), in close consultation with the Liberian National Malaria Control Program (NMCP) and with participation of nearly all national and international partners involved with malaria prevention and control in the country. The activities PMI is proposing conform to the Ministry of Health and Social Welfare (MOHSW)'s National Malaria Strategic Plan, and support investments made by the NMCP, Global Fund, United Nations Children's Emergency Fund (UNICEF), World Health Organization (WHO), and

---

[1] National Population and Housing Census, 2008 plus a growth rate of 2.1%

other donors to improve and expand malaria-related services. The proposed FY 2014 PMI funding of $12 million will support the following activities:

Insecticide-Treated Nets (ITNs): In its recent Strategic Plan, Liberia adopted a "universal coverage" goal for ITNs, defined operationally as one long-lasting insecticidal net (LLIN) for each sleeping space or a maximum of three LLINs per household. The country has set objectives of 90% of families receiving at least one LLIN, and at least 85% of the general population sleeping under LLINs. Current distribution approaches are through mass campaigns and antenatal services (ANC), reinforced by intense behavior change communication (BCC) at the community level. More than 4.5 million LLINs have been distributed in Liberia since 2008, including 1.7 million LLINs purchased and distributed by PMI. The 2011 MIS documented that 49% of households owned at least one LLIN.

The planned activities with FY 2014 funding include procurement and distribution of 327,700 LLINs. Most of these nets will support the NMCP's planned national universal coverage campaign in late 2014, while 18,160 nets will be set aside to close the estimated gap with the Global Fund for continuous distribution through antenatal clinics and institutional deliveries. PMI will also continue to support strengthening of the management of the national net program; improving logistics, forecasting, storage, distribution, and training; and behavior change communication activities to promote net usage as a community norm.

Indoor Residual Spraying (IRS) and Entomological Monitoring: PMI-supported IRS coverage expanded from approximately 22,000 structures (160,000 people) in 2009 to 96,901 structures (869,707 people) in 2012 with a coverage rate of 98% of targeted households. Also in 2012, resistance assays were conducted and used to inform insecticide selection for the 2013 spray round. Pyrethroid resistance was detected in 4 of 5 IRS counties, dictating a switch in insecticide to a long-lasting organophosphate. Due to the dramatically increased costs of non-pyrethroid based IRS, IRS will be suspended in Liberia after the 2013 spray round, and resources will be shifted to support LLIN procurements and increased entomological monitoring capacity.

With FY 2014 funding, PMI will support increased malaria surveillance and BCC in those districts where IRS is withdrawn. In addition PMI will help support the development of entomology capacity by providing equipment, supplies, training, and mentoring for NMCP entomology technicians to enable them to conduct mosquito density, behavior and resistance monitoring activities nationwide.

Malaria in Pregnancy (MIP): According to the 2011 MIS, 50% of pregnant women received two or more doses of IPTp during their last pregnancy. PMI continues to support the training of health workers and students in pre-service institutions. As part of this effort, in 2011 pre-service training materials for malaria in pregnancy (MIP) were finalized and printed. In addition, 432 general community health volunteers (gCHVs) were provided with comprehensive community health education materials that stress early antenatal care and prevention of MIP. In 2012, 289 gCHVs were trained. With FY 2014 funding, PMI will maintain support for capacity building of health staff for MIP and will support the distribution of MIP commodities, i.e., LLINs and sulfadoxine-pyrimethamine, through antenatal clinics. In addition, PMI will support an assessment of the policies and practices of the malaria in pregnancy program in Liberia, including the status of implementation of the revised WHO IPTp guidelines.

Case Management & Pharmaceutical Systems: The National Malaria Strategic Plan stresses parasitological diagnosis for all suspected malaria cases at both the facility and community level in Liberia. In 2012, only 22% of all reported malaria cases were clinically diagnosed. A transitional plan has been developed that will ensure that the National Diagnostics Unit of the MOHSW will assume responsibility for managing diagnostics in Liberia. With FY 2014 funding, PMI will procure laboratory supplies, including reagents for microscopy and rapid diagnostic tests (RDTs). PMI will also continue to support strengthening of the National Public Health Reference Laboratory and will support the NMCP's efforts to conduct refresher training for laboratory technicians.

In order to increase access to recommended malaria medications and encourage testing prior to treatment, the MOHSW has made RDTs and ACTs available to private sector health care facilities at no cost with the concomitant expectation that those facilities will report via the Health Management Information System (HMIS). At the community level, the ratio of gCHVs to community dwellers has increased to one gCHV for every 500 people. This has contributed to progress in diagnosing and treating uncomplicated malaria at the community level and to increased referrals of persistent febrile cases to health facilities.

In FY 2014 PMI will procure 1,117,000 ACT treatments to help fill Liberia's ACT needs. Quinine and artemether for treatment of severe malaria will also be procured. In addition, PMI will continue to support the extension of malaria case management to the community level and refresher training for facility-level case management. PMI will also support the Liberia Medicine and Health Product Regulatory Authority to provide quality assurance of antimalarials.

In 2013, Logistic Management Information System tools were increasingly used by health facilities in all the counties, and the Supply Chain Master Unit at the MOHSW recorded an increase in the reporting rate of consumption data. The storage and distribution of malaria commodities was also strengthened at the National Diagnostics Unit. With FY 2014 funds, PMI will continue to support strengthening of the drug and laboratory supply chain system at the central and county levels.

Monitoring & Evaluation: The NMCP has finalized and costed its M&E strategy and work plan. The Global Fund and PMI provide the bulk of the costs, while WHO provides technical support. The MOHSW has a fully integrated computerized HMIS that serves all public departments and programs and those private clinical facilities that receive medications and diagnostic support from the MOHSW. Personnel at all levels have been trained and the system is operational nationwide; however, reporting is not uniform and data are underutilized at all levels, primarily summarized for monthly reports to the next level. Some indicators also need to be revised to reflect updated policy and procedures. The main M&E activity during the last 12 months was the planning and implementation of the Demographic and Health Survey 2013 with a malaria module. No biomarkers were included. Results from the DHS 2013 will be available in early 2014.

With FY 2014 funds, PMI will support continued implementation of the End-Use Verification survey of the availability of malaria commodities at the health facility level. PMI will also provide resources for supportive supervision of M&E activities, for therapeutic efficacy monitoring, for the 2015 Malaria Indicator Survey, and for enhanced reporting and use of HMIS and LMIS data.

Behavior Change and Communication (BCC): During the past year, PMI has assisted the MOHSW in developing communication materials and in training and equipping health promoters to convey malaria messages. Six hundred and sixty eight gCHVs, trained traditional midwives, and community health promoters were trained to educate and engage communities on malaria. In addition, partnerships were arranged with five community radio stations for the airings of pre-recorded ITN use radio spot messages, and in collaboration with the Ministry of Education, schools introduced malaria messaging. With FY 2014 funds, PMI will support the implementation of integrated interpersonal communication activities, including health care worker training, and the implementation and monitoring of mass media malaria messages.

ACRONYMS

ACT	Artemisinin-based combination therapy
ANC	Antenatal care
BCC	Behavior change and communication
CDC	Centers for Disease Control and Prevention
CY	Calendar Year
DHS	Demographic and Health Survey
EPI	Expanded Program on Immunizations
EUV	End-Use Verification
FARA	Fixed Amount Reimbursement Agreement
FY	Fiscal year
gCHV	General community health volunteer
GHI	Global Health Initiative
Global Fund	Global Fund to Fight AIDS, Tuberculosis and Malaria
GOL	Government of Liberia
HCW	Health care worker
HFS	Health facility survey
HMIS	Health Management Information System
iCCM	Integrated community case management
IMCI	Integrated Management of Childhood Illnesses
IPTp	Intermittent preventive treatment during pregnancy
IRS	Indoor residual spraying
ITN	Insecticide-treated bed net
IVM	Integrated vector management
LIBR	Liberian Institute of Biomedical Research
LLIN	Long-lasting insecticide-treated mosquito net
LMHRA	Liberia Medicines and Health Products Regulatory Authority
LMIS	Logistics Management Information System
M&E	Monitoring and evaluation
MIP	Malaria in pregnancy
MIS	Malaria Indicator Survey
MOHSW	Ministry of Health & Social Welfare
MOP	Malaria Operational Plan
NDS	National Drug Service
NDU	National Diagnostics Unit
NGO	Non-governmental organization
NHSWPP	National Health and Social Welfare Policy and Plan
NMCP	National Malaria Control Program
NPHRL	National Public Health Reference Laboratory
PEMRAF	Public Financial Management Risk Assessment Framework
PEPFAR	President's Emergency Plan for AIDS Relief
PMI	President's Malaria Initiative
PQM	Promoting Quality Medicines
QA/QC	Quality assurance/quality control
RBM	Roll Back Malaria

RDT	Rapid diagnostic test
SLICE	Supply and Logistics Internal Control Evaluation
SP	Sulfadoxine-pyrimethamine
TA	Technical assistance
TTM	Trained traditional midwife
UNICEF	United Nations Children's Emergency Fund
USAID	United States Agency for International Development
USG	United States Government
WHO	World Health Organization

STRATEGY

1. Introduction

The President's Malaria Initiative (PMI) is a major component of the United States Government's (USG's) effort to prevent and control malaria in sub-Saharan Africa. PMI was launched in June 2005 as a 5-year program with funding of $1.2 billion and a goal to reduce malaria-related mortality by 50%. The strategy for achieving this goal was to reach 85% coverage of the most vulnerable groups – children under five years of age and pregnant women – with evidence-based preventive and therapeutic interventions, including artemisinin-based combination therapies (ACTs), insecticide-treated bed nets (ITNs), intermittent preventive treatment during pregnancy (IPTp), and indoor residual spraying (IRS). Owing to PMI's progress, in 2008 the Lantos-Hyde Act extended funding for PMI and the PMI strategy was revised to achieve Africa-wide impact by halving the burden of malaria in 70 percent of at-risk populations in sub-Saharan Africa. In 2008, Liberia became PMI's eighth focus country. Funding for PMI activities in Liberia has ranged from $11.8 million to $18.0 million annually between FY 2008 and FY 2014.

In implementing PMI, the USG works closely with host governments and within existing national malaria control plans. Efforts are also coordinated with other national and international partners, including the Global Fund to Fight AIDS, Tuberculosis, and Malaria (Global Fund), Roll Back Malaria (RBM), and the World Bank's Malaria Booster Program, as well as non-governmental organizations and the private sector, to ensure that investments are complementary and that host country, RBM, and Millennium Development goals and objectives are achieved. PMI aims to ensure that all country assessment, evaluation, and planning sessions are inclusive, transparent, and collaborative. Over the past few years in Liberia, PMI has strengthened coordination and collaboration among donors, particularly with the Global Fund.

The Liberian Ministry of Health and Social Welfare's (MOHSW) National Malaria Control Program (NMCP) has made progress in decreasing malaria-related mortality. However, challenges remain. This section of Liberia's Malaria Operational Plan (MOP) FY 2014: 1) briefly reviews the current status of interventions; 2) identifies challenges, opportunities, and threats that pose barriers to the progress of activities under PMI; and 3) lays out a strategic plan to achieve high impact results within an environment of shrinking financial resources.

2. Malaria Situation in Liberia

Liberia covers 43,000 square miles in West Africa and is bounded by nearly 350 miles of Atlantic Ocean off the southwest and by the neighboring countries of Sierra Leone (northwest), Guinea (north) and Côte d'Ivoire (east and southeast). Most of the country lies at altitudes below 500 meters. The coastal areas are characterized by mangrove swamps, which give way to tropical rain forest that gradually thins out northwards to be replaced by deciduous forest. All geographic areas of Liberia are favorable to malaria transmission. Liberia has hyper-/holoendemic malaria.

The major vectors for malaria are *Anopheles gambiae* s.s, *An. funestus*, and *An. melas*. The major parasite species are *Plasmodium falciparum* (>90%), *P. ovale*, and *P. malariae.*[2]

According to results from the 2005 Malaria Indicator Survey (MIS), the prevalence of malaria parasitemia in children under five was 66%. The prevalence rate fell to 32% in 2009, and was 28% according to the 2011 MIS. The geographical prevalence of malaria according to the 2011 MIS is shown in the map below.

Prevalence of Malaria Parasitemia in Children under Five Years of Age by Region, Liberia 2011 MIS

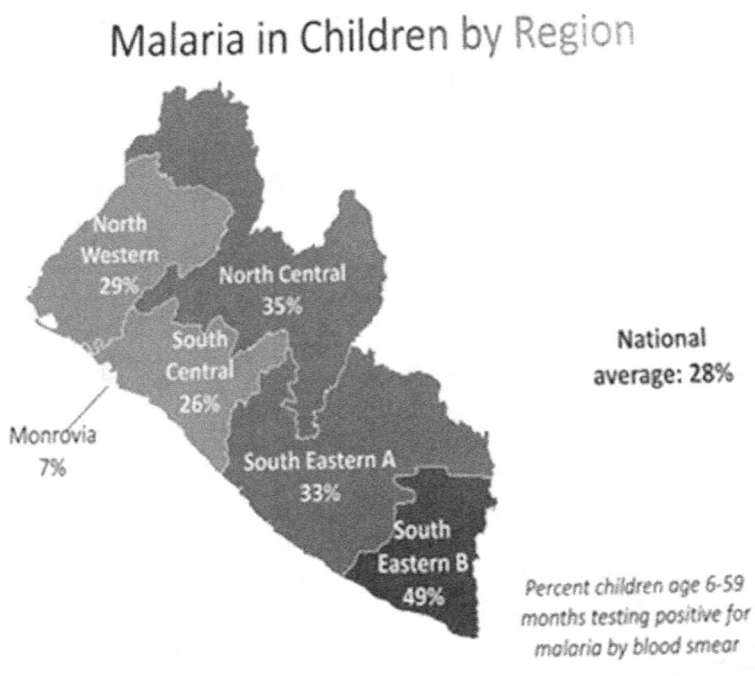

The entire population of approximately 3.8 million[3] is at risk of the disease; children under five and pregnant women are the most affected groups. According to reports received by the WHO in 2010 from the NMCP, approximately 40% of consultations in outpatient departments in all age groups in public health facilities are due to malaria.[4] The 2009 Health Facility Survey estimates that malaria accounts for 33% of in-patient deaths.

Since August 2005, Liberia has made considerable progress in malaria control and prevention. The achievements from August 2005 to 2011 documented in the 2011 MIS include:

---

[2] Roll Back Malaria-National Desk Analysis-Liberia- 2001
[3] National Population and Housing Census, 2008 plus a growth rate of 2.1%
[4] http://www.aho.afro.who.int/profiles_information/index.php/File:Reported_malaria_cases_by_county.PNG

- 50% of households have at least one ITN, up from 18% in 2005[5]
- 37% of children under five slept under an ITN the previous night, up from 2.6% in 2005
- 39% of pregnant women slept under an ITN the previous night; in 2005 31% of women slept under any type of net
- 50% of women received two or more IPTp doses during their most recent pregnancy, up from 4.5% in 2005
- 25% of children under five received an ACT treatment for malaria within 24 hours from the onset of fever, up from 5% in 2005.

3. National Malaria Control Strategy

The GOL/MOHSW's Liberian Malaria Control Strategy for 2010-2015 aims to sustain progress in reducing malaria-related mortality, scale-up the most effective malaria control and prevention activities from the health facility to the community level, and involve all partners (including the private sector) in supporting health care delivery.

Under the 2010-2015 Liberia Malaria Control Strategy, the NMCP assumes the lead coordination role and takes responsibility for the decentralization of malaria control and prevention activities throughout the country by gradually devolving implementation responsibilities to County Health and Social Welfare Teams. This coordination role includes all health partners, donors, and private sector stakeholders.

Malaria control and prevention activities in Liberia follow the principle of the "three ones":

- One national malaria control coordinating authority where implementation is a country-led process;
- One comprehensive plan for malaria control, including costed work plans; and
- One country-level monitoring and evaluation framework.

The four basic technical pillars or strategic interventions are:

1. *Case management through improved malaria treatment and the scale up of ACTs.* Resources are to be directed towards increasing the availability and use of malaria diagnostic tools and artemisinin-based combination therapies (ACTs) as first-line treatment in all public health facilities, at the community level, and in the private sector. To ensure quality of care, training will focus on strengthening key providers' skills. Malaria treatment guidelines will be revised to ensure coordinated implementation at all levels. National targets include:

- At least 80% of patients with uncomplicated malaria receive early diagnosis and prompt and effective treatment according to MOHSW guidelines; and
- At least 65% of patients with complicated or severe malaria are diagnosed in a timely manner and receive correct treatment according to MOHSW guidelines.

---

[5] Liberia Malaria Indicator Survey, 2005

2. *Integrated Vector Management (IVM) to prevent mosquito-to-human contact, to reduce vector abundance, and to improve environmental sanitation and control of potential breeding sites.* IVM in Liberia includes the provision of long-lasting insecticide-treated nets (LLINs) through mass distribution to all households and targeted distribution to pregnant women and children under five. The strategy also includes targeted indoor residual spraying (IRS) for sleeping structures and targeted larviciding. In its Strategic Plan and Operational Guidelines on Long-Lasting Insecticidal Nets for Liberia 2012-2017, Liberia adopted a "universal coverage" goal for ITNs, defined operationally as one LLIN for each sleeping space or a maximum of three LLINs per household.

National targets include:

- At least 90% of families have received at least one LLIN;
- At least 85% of children and pregnant women sleep under LLINs;
- At least 85% of the general population sleep under LLINs; and
- At least 85% of the population in targeted districts is protected by IRS.

3. *Malaria prevention and control during pregnancy.* Since the introduction of intermittent preventive treatment during pregnancy (IPTp) in Liberia in 2004, the use of sulfadoxine-pyrimethamine (SP) for malaria during pregnancy has been gradually increasing, paralleling the gradual increase in access to health care. Trained traditional midwives are expected to refer pregnant women to ANC clinics rather than supply IPTp at the community level. However, for pregnant women residing more than five kilometers from ANC services, certified midwives deliver ANC services, including SP, while also encouraging early and repeated ANC clinic attendance. National targets include:

- At least 80% of pregnant women attending antenatal consultation receive IPTp according to the national MIP protocol;
- 80% of all pregnant women diagnosed with malaria at health facilities (public or private) receive prompt and effective treatment according to national treatment protocol;
- All pregnant women with suspected malaria at the community level are referred to the nearest health facility and receive prompt and effective treatment; and
- At least 80% of pregnant women attending antenatal consultation receive an LLIN.

4. *Support for advocacy, social mobilization, and behavior change communication (BCC).* This component will focus on the role of health providers and the community in malaria control and prevention activities, using a multichannel approach for health education with emphasis on radio messages, community health volunteers, and child-to-child communication. Key change agents for dissemination of malaria messages will include peer educators, trained care-givers, and other locally respected authorities. National targets include:

- All health facilities (public and private) provide updated malaria health education; and
- 90% of the population has heard a malaria message through multimedia channels.

The above four technical pillars in turn rest on a foundation of support functions designed to facilitate their effective rollout and implementation in a cross-cutting manner.

- **M&E and Research**: Monitoring and evaluation is a major focus of both the MOHSW and the NMCP. The NMCP has developed a comprehensive M&E plan in collaboration with the M&E unit of the Department of Planning at the MOHSW and with other technical partners. This plan will be integrated with the health management and information system (HMIS) of the MOHSW. More detailed operational M&E plans will be prepared on an annual basis and revised when necessary. Malaria-specific indicators will be selected from the RBM core indicators, as well as program-specific indicators to measure performance. All data collected (routine and surveys) will be analyzed, and reports will be produced and shared with stakeholders.
- **Supply Chain Management**: Supply chain management continues to be one of the biggest challenges facing health care programs in Liberia. Inadequate storage, inventory and warehouse management practices, and limited information sharing continue to contribute to stockouts of commodities and uncertain drug quality. The NMCP and the public health community see this activity as a key priority.
- **Program Management and Administration**: In order to ensure that the NMCP is able to provide expert advice on malaria prevention and control activities in Liberia, additional capacity building, particularly in program management and M&E are required. This capacity building will be a continuous process that will provide the NMCP with the technical capabilities, resources, and information needed to carry out its responsibilities, including fostering effective partnerships among stakeholders.

The election of President Ellen Johnson Sirleaf as the chairperson of the African Leaders Malaria Alliance (ALMA) in 2012 brought additional political support to the fight against malaria in Liberia.

4. PMI Goals and Objectives

The goal of PMI is to halve the burden of malaria in 70 percent of at-risk populations in sub-Saharan Africa. By the end of 2014, PMI will assist Liberia to achieve the following targets in populations at risk for malaria:

- >90% of households with a pregnant woman and/or children under five will own at least one ITN;
- 85% of children under five will have slept under an ITN the previous night;
- 85% of pregnant women will have slept under an ITN the previous night;
- 85% of houses in geographic areas targeted for IRS will have been sprayed;

- 85% of pregnant women and children under five will have slept under an ITN the previous night or in a house that has been sprayed with IRS in the last six months;
- 85% of women who have completed a pregnancy in the last two years will have received two or more doses of IPTp during that pregnancy;
- 85% of government health facilities will have ACTs available for treatment of uncomplicated malaria; and
- 85% of children under five with suspected malaria will have received treatment with ACTs within 24 hours of onset of their symptoms.

5. Progress on Indicators to Date

The most up-to-date information on the status of malaria prevention and control interventions in Liberia comes from Malaria Indicator Surveys (MIS) funded by PMI. The table below shows progress since the 2005 MIS and results from the 2011 MIS.

Progress on Indicators to Date

CORE INDICATORS	RBM Targets 2010	PMI Targets 2014	MIS 2005	MIS 2009	MIS 2011
Proportion of all households that own at least one ITN	85%	90%	18%	47%	50%
Proportion of children <5 who slept under an ITN the previous night	80%	85%	2.6%	27%	37%
Proportion of pregnant women who slept under an ITN the previous night	80%	85%	n/a	33%	39%
Proportion of pregnant women and children <5 who slept under an ITN the previous night or in a house that has been sprayed with IRS in the last 6 months	n/a	85%	n/a	n/a	W=45% <5=43%
Proportion of women who have completed a pregnancy in the last two years and received two or more doses of IPTp during their pregnancy	80%	85%	4.5%	45%	50%
Proportion of children <5 suspected with malaria who received ACTs within 24h of onset of their symptoms.	80%	85%	5.3%	17%	24.5%
Proportion of children <5 with any kind of anemia (severe anemia)	n/a	n/a	87%	63% (5%)	n/a (8%)
Proportion of children with positive parasitemia among children <5	n/a	n/a	66%	32%	28%

6. Other Relevant Evidence on Progress

The 2009 Health Facility Survey also provides useful information on the progress of facility-based malaria activities. A total of 418 health facilities, representing 79% of all health facilities in Liberia, were visited, and the survey included record review, assessment of commodities, and observation of malaria case management. Results from the Health Facility Survey are encouraging, as 86% of health workers were prescribing antimalarial drugs according to national guidelines and 85% of health workers had access to essential malaria drugs.

Key Indicators of the Liberia Health Facility Surveys

	INDICATORS	HFS 2005	HFS 2009
1	% of GOL health facilities that have all four presentation of ACTs available for treatment of uncomplicated malaria on the day of visit	58	71
2	% of health workers who search for danger signs	11	20
3	% of health workers who prescribe antimalarial drug according to national guidelines	75	86
4	% of health workers who counsel of patients/caretakers on malaria	26	45
5	% of health workers with access to essential malaria drugs	48	85
6	% of out-patient department attendance due to malaria among children under five years	59*	38
7	% of pregnant women with confirmed malaria	31	18
8	% of patients receiving appropriate malaria treatment within 24 hours	21	35
9	% of overall deaths with laboratory-confirmed malaria (rapid diagnostic test or blood smear)	44	33

* Clinical malaria

7. Integration, Collaboration, Coordination

The Global Health Initiative (GHI) is the USG vehicle for ensuring all USG global health investments are efficiently coordinated with recipient countries' health priorities in order to achieve maximum ownership and results. Thus, the guiding principle of the USG's GHI strategy for Liberia is to ensure all USG health investments align with Liberia's 2011-2021 National Health and Social Welfare Policy and Plan (NHSWPP), which is designed to expand access to basic health services and to establish the building blocks of equitable, effective, responsive, and sustainable health service delivery. The USG complements the Liberian MOHSW's efforts by concentrating its resources on two key focus areas: 1) improving service delivery through the Essential Package of Health Services and 2) strengthening health systems to increase institutional capacity and sustainability.

Through GHI the USG will invest in capacity building and technical assistance for policy formulation, strategy development, health systems strengthening, and countrywide BCC initiatives. Additionally, the USG is using MOHSW systems to provide both facility-based and community-based support under performance-based contracting with NGOs for specific health facilities and their catchment communities. The USG is also providing complementary technical assistance for quality assurance, in-service training, and supportive supervision.

Performance-based contracting is a service agreement entered into between the MOHSW and NGOs to carry out service delivery at health facilities and catchment communities. These NGOs are expected to ensure health care services are in consonance with the Essential Package of Health Services, which is a standard government-approved package for primary health care services in Liberia. These contracts include a performance bonus for reaching targets on quantity and quality indicators after verification of submitted data at the county level and counter-verification by the central level committee comprised of the MOHSW and third party stakeholders.

From 2005 until 2007, the Global Fund constituted the majority of external funding for the implementation of malaria control and prevention activities in Liberia. A $37 million Global Fund Round 7 grant was signed in April 2008, with the United Nations Development Program as the Principal Recipient, and in 2011 a $60 million Round 10 grant was signed with the MOHSW and an NGO, Plan Liberia, as the two Principal Recipients. Currently, the MOHSW and Plan Liberia manage a consolidated grant of Round 7 Phase 2 and Round 10 Phase 1.

In 2010, PMI helped create a Donors Forum to coordinate malaria donors' efforts and prevent duplication. The forum included the WHO, UNICEF, and the Global Fund. A key achievement of the forum was the formulation of a joint 2011 annual work plan developed by the NMCP to monitor the activities of partners and provide a platform for further collaboration. This has resulted in increased collaboration, coordination, and integration among partners supporting the NMCP.

In Liberia, PMI prioritizes the scale-up of integrated community case management (iCCM) to increase access to health services at the community level, and in collaboration with UNICEF, PMI supports the Community Health Services Division of the MOHSW to implement iCCM. This program provides treatment for malaria, diarrhea, and acute respiratory infections for children under five at the community level. The Global Fund, under its Round 10 grant, has committed support to the expansion of the iCCM program nationwide.

The MOHSW has prioritized the integration of diagnostic capacity for malaria, tuberculosis, and HIV at the central and regional levels. The MOHSW established a National Diagnostics Unit (NDU) to coordinate the support of partners to maintain achievements and continue progress. PMI and other USAID programs are coordinating with the NDU, the Global Fund, and other partners to operationalize an integrated diagnostics strategy that will provide comprehensive diagnostic policies, standard operational guidelines, and a national diagnostic program for Liberia.

Another NGO, the MENTOR Initiative, is supporting a pilot in the greater Monrovia area of Montserrado County to provide ACTs to the private sector (i.e., wholesalers and retailers) for increased access to malaria treatment. This pilot will provide access to 57% of the population that seek treatment for malaria from private pharmacies, medicine shops, and health facilities. PMI has provided technical input to the NMCP, and based on results and lessons learned, the Global Fund will support the scale-up of this pilot private sector activity to the rest of the country through a Round 10 grant.

Additionally, PMI, in collaboration with the NMCP, has initiated a partnership with private companies to support the continued implementation of IRS. Under this initiative, the Arcelor Mittal Steel Company has conducted two rounds of spraying in its concession areas in Nimba and Grand Bassa Counties. The Liberia Agriculture Company has also been engaged in this public-private partnership and has supported one round of spraying in its concessional area in Grand Bassa County. PMI has provided insecticides and technical support, including training and mentoring, to these companies to build capacity to conduct IRS. As these companies increase their financial support to conduct IRS, PMI will decrease its support and shift resources towards strengthening the vector control and entomological capacity of the NMCP in collaboration with the U.S. Naval Medical Research Unit No. 3 (NAMRU-3), which has been surveying mosquito populations at sentinel sites in Liberia since 2011.

8. PMI Support Strategy

The overall PMI support strategy for Liberia is nested within the GHI strategy for Liberia, which seeks to align, complement, and support Liberia's 2011-2021 NHSWPP. To improve the overall health status of the population, strategic investments need to be made that take the best advantage of resources from government, development partners, and technical agencies.

PMI's national-level support includes health system strengthening, bolstering the Health Management Information System (HMIS), improving pharmaceutical and commodity supply chain management, and enhancing BCC activities. Diagnostics, promoting quality medicines, ITN distribution through ANC clinics, and the provision of antimalarial commodities in health facilities, are among specific interventions that PMI will continue to support under its nationwide investment approach. In many cases, PMI is one partner among several others, enabling PMI to expand its activities beyond what could have been possible otherwise.

Support at the county level consists of the implementation of Liberia's Essential Package of Health Services at the facility and community levels through a government-to-government Fixed Amount Reimbursement Agreement (FARA). This is the principal delivery mechanism for preventive and curative malaria activities. Up to three counties will be targeted for service delivery and an additional three counties will be targeted for strategic support to augment service delivery and decentralized system strengthening. These counties were prioritized based on their population concentration (the six counties account for 75% of the total population of Liberia) and their potential to fuel nationwide development. Several USAID funding streams including HIV/AIDS, maternal and child health, and family planning, will be combined with PMI resources. Scale-up to nationwide coverage for all activities, except IRS, will be achieved through coordination with the Global Fund, the multi-donor Pool Fund, and the European Union.

Accountability of PMI resources at the county level will be through MOHSW performance-based contracting of NGOs. There are seven malaria specific indicators used to assess the performance of contracted NGOs under the FARA: management of malaria according to the standard malaria protocol, management of uncomplicated malaria, management of complicated malaria, availability of mosquito nets for ANC, availability of RDTs, availability of ACTs, and availability of SP. USAID visits each FARA county every quarter and randomly selects facilities for field monitoring. USAID uses baseline assessment documents and integrated supervision monitoring reports provided by the county health teams and partners to verify performance of the various health facilities under the FARA. In addition, HMIS indicators may be used evaluate the FARA, as both IPTp and treatment indicators are included as indicators in the PBF scheme. To date, HMIS data shows continued improvements in service delivery within counties supported through the FARA, as well as those supported by other donors. For instance, IPTp-2 coverage among pregnant women residing in catchment areas around USAID-supported facilities in Bong in 2012 was 79%, up from 70% the previous year. In Lofa, IPTp went from 45% to 58%.

9. Challenges, Opportunities, and Threats

Significant strides remain to be made to reduce malaria-related morbidity and mortality in Liberia. The main challenges include: 1) inefficient supply chain management; 2) inadequate Logistics Management Information System (LMIS) reporting and use; 3) need for greater capacity at the NMCP for managerial and supervisory functions; and 4) budget constraints.

Since its inception in 2008, PMI has allocated an average 40% of its annual budget to the procurement and distribution of antimalarial commodities. The supply chain for these commodities, particularly for ACTs and RDTs, is critical for diagnosis and treatment of malaria. Although the MOHSW developed a Supply Chain Master Plan in 2010 (with technical assistance from PEPFAR), the implementation of the plan continues to stall due to limited and inadequate financial, human, and material resources. This delay has resulted in persistent stockouts of antimalarial commodities in health facilities. Through the Donors Forum, PMI continues to coordinate with the Global Fund to harness the required funding and human capacity necessary to implement the Supply Chain Master Plan.

The LMIS data emanating from health facilities should feed into the database of the Supply Chain Management Unit of the MOHSW to inform forecasting, quantification, and procurement planning of health commodities. However, data quality remains unreliable and continues to make forecasting and quantification difficult. The NMCP has recognized these problems and has increased its coordination with PMI to remedy the situation. Additionally, the Global Fund has committed resources to the rollout of the LMIS forms to eleven counties, complementing the effort of PMI in the four largest counties. Currently, the NMCP is engaged in an independent assessment of the situation surrounding stockouts of antimalarial commodities in collaboration with the National Drug Service, the county depots, and selected health facilities.

The NMCP has the opportunity moving forward to track performance and implementation through its newly revised and costed M&E Strategic Plan, but the managerial and supervisory capacity at the NMCP should be bolstered in order to ensure the long-term sustainability of malaria activities. Two of the NMCP's most effective personnel were recently promoted to higher-level positions within the MOHSW; replacement of these individuals will require managerial training to meet the increasing demands for program oversight and efficiency from the NMCP.

The GOL has gradually increased its national budget allocation for health sector activities from $10 million in 2006/2007 to $70 million in 2012/2013. However, there is still a heavy reliance on donor support for health services delivery, and budget constraints threaten the level of support that will be provided in the future. In addition, the rising costs of IRS due to insecticide resistance will necessitate a shift to universal LLIN coverage as the primary vector control intervention in former IRS-targeted districts in Liberia in calendar year 2014. It is incumbent upon the GOL to absorb more of the country's health expenditures.

10. Updates in Strategy since Last Year

PMI and the Global Fund are the main donors that support malaria activities in Liberia. Phase 1 of Liberia's Round 10 Global Fund grant is drawing to a close in 2013; therefore, the MOHSW/NMCP and the other Principal Recipient, PLAN Liberia, have been occupied with completing the assessment of Phase 1 and the application for Phase 2 renewal. PMI has supported the NMCP and other parties in these efforts by providing technical assistance, particularly regarding the quantification of commodities. As PMI complements the activities under the Global Fund, PMI will support long-term technical assistance for Global Fund grant implementation. A terms of reference is currently being finalized for a malaria advisor to be seconded to the NMCP, and it is hoped that the position will be filled to help support Phase 2 implementation.

A key element of the Global Fund renewal involves the NMCP's plan for a nationwide, coordinated distribution of LLINs in late 2014. This is a change from the previous strategy of rolling distribution, in which different parts of the country received nets in different campaigns. Although more challenging logistically and financially, a nationwide LLIN campaign would help the country reach its goal of universal LLIN coverage. The bulk of the needed nets are included in the Global Fund application; the focus for PMI would be to ensure routine distribution continues through ANC clinics and to women who deliver at institutions.

PMI is providing technical assistance to the NMCP in various technical areas and program management, particularly while the Deputy Program Manager at the NMCP is also functioning as the Acting Program Manager. The position of Program Director was being advertised during the MOP team visit and the Minister of Health specifically mentioned his intention to move quickly to fill this key leadership position for the NMCP.

OPERATIONAL PLAN

1. Insecticide-Treated Nets (ITNs)

NMCP/PMI Objectives

In its Strategic Plan and Operational Guidelines on Long-Lasting Insecticidal Nets for Liberia 2012-2017, Liberia adopted a "universal coverage" goal for ITNs, defined operationally as one LLIN for each sleeping space or a maximum of three LLINs per household. The country has set objectives of 90% of families receiving at least one LLIN, and at least 85% of the general population sleeping under LLINs. Current distribution approaches are through mass campaigns and continuous antenatal care (ANC) services, reinforced by intense behavior change communication (BCC) at the community level.

Liberia was one of the first countries to distribute LLINs door-to-door through campaigns in combination with net "hang-up" in households. To date, the country has implemented a phased strategy by county, aiming to replenish nets every three years. More than 4.5 million LLINs have been distributed in Liberia since 2008, including 1.7 million LLINs purchased by PMI. Records of geographic distributions by county are incomplete. The ITN distributions shown in the table below may reflect only certain districts or communities rather than full counties, with campaigns and ANC combined. Nevertheless, these records may indicate counties where nets were not replaced as needed after three years, and an inconsistent allocation of nets by county over time. In late 2014, the NMCP plans to conduct its first ever, national mass LLIN distribution campaign.

By the time the country had conducted its last Malaria Indicator Survey (MIS) in 2011, approximately 1.7 million nets distributed during 2009-2010 should still have been viable. Yet the MIS documented only a small increase in household ownership of nets; 49% of households had at least one LLIN, up from 47% in the 2009 MIS. While noting a marked improvement over the household net ownership levels of 18% in the 2005 MIS and 30% in the 2007 DHS, the NMCP and partners had expected a larger increase. The NMCP received anecdotal reports that some people may have hidden nets during the survey hoping to receive a new one, resold them in markets, or sent them across counties and international borders. A PMI-supported qualitative assessment of ownership of mass distribution campaign nets planned for late 2013 will help confirm these reports and explore other possible reasons for low LLIN ownership.

The 2011 MIS estimates for ITN use among children under five and pregnant women were 37% and 39%, respectively. Encouragingly, the MIS also showed that in households *owning* an ITN, 68% and 77% respectively slept under an ITN the previous night, up from 51% and 60% in the 2009 MIS. These data seem to indicate that most people will use nets if they are available; thus, access and ownership are keys to ensuring actual use.

The NMCP also aims to complement campaigns with continuous distribution of nets during the first ANC visit, at delivery in a health care institution to encourage delivery in facilities, and through the Expanded Program on Immunization (EPI). ANC distribution has just begun; a supply of nets from the Global Fund for approximately six months was distributed to all counties in February 2013. Distribution of LLINs during delivery at a health facility has also begun. Distribution through EPI clinics has not yet begun.

LLIN Distribution by County through Campaigns and Antenatal Clinics, Liberia, 2008-2012

County	Pop 2008	2008	2009	2010	2011	2012	Cumulative since 2008
Bomi	84,119	83,100 (PMI)	--	1,200	43,300	88,194 (Global Fund)	215,794
Bong	333,481	212,400 (UNICEF)	--	3,300	113,600	210,035 (Global Fund)	539,335
Gbarpolu	83,388	--	54,408	1,260	--	50,977 (PMI)	106,645
Grand Bassa	221,693	32,000	132,000 (PMI)	1,950	45,900	177,014 (Global Fund)	388,864
Grand Cape Mount	127,706	113,900 (PMI)	--	1,950	--	92,000 (PMI)	207,850
Grand Gedeh	125,258	51,500 (Germany)	--	1,900	83,000 (incl. PMI)	--	136,400
Grand Kru	57,913	16,500	9,900	3,900	24,300 (incl. PMI)	--	54,600
Lofa	276,863	--	120,100 (PMI)	2,800	76,700	185,443 (Global Fund)	385,043
Margibi	209,923	--	141,759	2,000 (Global Fund)	--	149,126 (PMI) 37,178 (Global Fund)	330,063
Maryland	135,938	66,900 (Germany)	23,600	2,000	87,100 (incl. PMI)	--	179,600
Montserrado	1,118,241	--	76,154	846,540 (incl. PMI)	125,000 (incl. PMI)	3,850 (PMI), 143,743 (Global Fund)	1,195,287
Nimba	462,026	--	177,900 (PMI)	11,000 (includes PMI)	120,500	157,811 (Global Fund)	467,211
River Cess	71,509	45,000 (Germany)	31,870	1,000	43,800 (incl. PMI)	--	121,670
River Gee	66,789	32,800	15,800	1,000	28,400 (incl. PMI)	--	78,000
Sinoe	102,391	36,500 (Germany)	29,217	1,600	38,400 (incl. PMI)	--	69,217
Total distributed by year	n/a	690,600	812,708	883,400	830,000	1,295,371	4,512,079
Totals procured by PMI each year	n/a	197,000	430,000	480,000	350,000	300,000	1,757,000

Sources: NMCP Strategic Plan and Operational Guidelines for LLINs in Liberia 2012-2017; Plan International, LLIN Distribution Report March 29, 2013; Liberia Red Cross Society reports 2011. Donor support indicated where known.

Progress during last 12 months

Two significant mass campaigns occurred in 2012. The first, with PMI support, was conducted in four counties in February and March 2012. Of 300,000 LLINs procured, teams distributed a total of 295,953 nets, covering hotels, ANC clinics, and inpatient health facilities in Montserrado, and health facilities and communities in Margibi, Grand Cape Mount, and Gbarpolu counties. A community-based evaluation immediately after the distribution found that 90% of households had at least one net, and 68% of children under the age of five had slept under a net the previous night. The NMCP and Plan Liberia coordinated the second mass distribution in November to December 2012, with funding from the Global Fund Consolidated Grant Phase 1. Community health volunteers distributed nearly 997,000 nets in 33 health districts in 7 counties (representing 58% of all health districts in those counties). After meeting their distribution targets, about 99,000 surplus nets were returned for distribution through ANC. Inadequate monitoring and inconsistent communications during the Global Fund campaign may have compromised the quality of hang-up activities. A post-campaign survey of the December 2012 mass distribution is not scheduled, though the 2013 DHS in progress will help measure campaign outcomes.

PMI supported two important consultations to help improve LLIN distribution strategies and implementation. A Supply and Logistics Internal Control Evaluation (SLICE) was conducted in part to identify problems that may contribute to low LLIN ownership rates despite past distributions. The SLICE team assessed the NMCP's management and logistics systems for both campaigns and continuous ITN distribution. They observed significant challenges with clarifying governance structures and standard operating procedures, ensuring consistent stakeholder interpretations of campaign guidance, resolving supply shortages in campaign and ANC settings, and providing adequate warehouse security. The team recommended improving planning and documentation procedures, fostering better coordination among stakeholders for supply chain systems, creating a Project Management Office, and developing a comprehensive campaign manual, among others.

In addition, PMI sponsored a workshop for the NMCP and partners to identify strategies and quantities for continuous distribution of LLINs. Modeling scenarios incorporated coverage and census data and reported net distribution. The participants concluded that the current continuous distribution through ANC would not achieve and sustain the 85% household ownership objective over time following mass campaigns. New continuous distribution approaches to explore include distribution through EPI clinics, schools, and community and retail channels. While it is agreed that efforts for the time being should be focused on achieving a high quality mass campaign, the NMCP will begin to use the modeling tool with further PMI support to develop a national strategy on continuous distribution for LLINs. It is likely that the NMCP will commit to strengthening the ANC channel, but they will need support to articulate their plans for other continuous distribution methods.

Challenges, opportunities, and threats

The NMCP and partners agree that the LLIN distribution system for both campaign and continuous channels faces significant challenges: poor supply chain management, inadequate donor coordination, weak tracking of net distribution by county, sporadic coverage of districts and counties, and slow implementation of distribution through ANC, all lead to disappointing progress toward achieving targets for ownership and use. Citing these constraints, the NMCP opted to revise its strategy and plan its first ever, national mass LLIN distribution campaign in late 2014, which will ensure that all districts are targeted. Given limited resources for indoor residual spraying (IRS), the NMCP wants to ensure that every household is covered by at least one vector control method.

Gap analysis

Gap Analysis for ITNs, Liberia CY 2012 – 2016 (as of July 2013)

Need	2012	2013	2014	2015	2016
Campaign distribution			2,195,796		
Continuous distribution: ANC and institutional delivery		245,430*	272,718	294,587	317,254
Total need		**245,430**	**2,468,514**	**294,587**	**317,254**
Committed or distributed and funding source - campaigns					
PMI MOP FY 2010-2011	300,000				
PMI MOP FY 2013			250,000		
PMI MOP FY 2014			309,540		
Global Fund Consolidated Grant	884,600		909,089		
Carry-over from 2013			71,578		
Total campaign committed or distributed	**1,184,600**		**1,540,207**		
Committed or distributed and funding source - continuous					
PMI MOP FY 2014 (ANC and institutional delivery)				18,160	
Global Fund Consolidated Grant (ANC and institutional delivery)		334,794	254,932	276,427	
Carry-over from 2013			17,786		
Total continuous committed or distributed		**334,794**	**272,718**	**294,587**	
ANNUAL CAMPAIGN GAP			655,589		
ANNUAL CONTINUOUS GAP (SURPLUS)		(89,364)	0	0	317,254
TOTAL ANNUAL LLIN GAP (SURPLUS)		(89,364)	655,589	0	317,254

* Based on 5% expected pregnant women in a year
Source: NMCP Global Fund-Roll Back Malaria Gap Analysis 2013

Plans and justification

The NMCP's new strategy to increase LLIN coverage provides an excellent opportunity for PMI and other partners to support the NMCP to plan and implement a high-quality national campaign. The NMCP and partners will advocate for resources to procure the nearly 2.2 million nets needed to achieve universal coverage. However, the current strategy of door-to-door distribution plus hang-up may prove logistically challenging and expensive to implement on a national scale. The NMCP's parallel commitment to develop a more robust continuous distribution strategy provides an opportunity to scale-up current distribution through ANC facilities and incorporate new approaches. In addition, findings and recommendations from the SLICE report could serve as a framework for strengthening the LLIN supply chain management system for both campaigns and continuous services.

Proposed activities with FY 2014 funding ($2,236,500)

- Procure LLINs. PMI will procure about 327,700 LLINs for distribution through mass campaigns and continuous services. Most of these nets will support the NMCP's planned national campaign in late 2014. These nets will complement PMI's 250,000 nets procured with FY 2013 funding and the 909,089 nets being proposed under the Global Fund Consolidated Phase 2 grant. PMI will work with the NMCP to identify other funding sources to cover the estimated 655,589 of the nearly 2.2 million nets needed to achieve universal coverage (see above gap analysis). PMI will also reprogram FY 2013 funds to support a technical advisor in country to help the NMCP and partners plan and implement the campaign. Should the campaign net gap not be filled, PMI will advise the NMCP and partners on alternative ways to distribute the nets committed to achieve the highest impact. For example, the NMCP could prioritize highly endemic rural counties that received nets three or more years ago and must have nets replaced, and those where IRS operations have ended. In effect, this would then become a phased campaign, although that is not the preference of the NMCP. In addition, PMI will set aside 18,160 nets to close the remaining estimated gap with the Global Fund for continuous distribution in 2015. ($1,474,650)

- Distribute LLINs. PMI will support LLIN distribution through local NGOs, including warehousing, transportation, training of supervisors, and monitoring of activities. PMI will work with the NMCP to address the issues of supply management identified in the 2012 SLICE assessment. ($573,850)

- Technical assistance for continuous distribution planning. As a follow-up to the workshop in 2012, PMI will fund technical assistance to help the NMCP begin framing a national strategy for distributing LLINs through continuous channels. The technical advisor will help assess options such as child immunization clinics, schools, and other mechanisms to maintain coverage after campaigns. ($188,000)

2. Indoor Residual Spraying and Entomological Monitoring

NMCP/PMI Objectives

The 2010-2015 revised NMCP strategy includes increased use of IRS in rural districts of high malaria prevalence, covering approximately 50% of the population, in order to quickly reduce malaria transmission. IRS is used to complement LLINs to reduce malaria prevalence, morbidity, and mortality.

Progress during last 12 months

In 2012, IRS was conducted in 96,901 eligible structures (comprising 98% of targeted households), thus protecting 869,707 people living in 14 districts of five counties.[6] Additionally, resistance assays were conducted to inform insecticide selection for the 2013 IRS campaign. The assay results confirmed resistance to pyrethroid insecticides among local mosquitoes in four IRS counties. Therefore, it was recommended that the spraying program switch to a long-lasting organophosphate for the next spray season (see the table below for susceptibility testing results).

Summary of 2012 Susceptibility Studies on *Anopheles gambiae* s.l. against three classes of insecticide in IRS counties, Liberia

Month	County (District)	Insecticide	Number Tested	24-Hour Mortality
May	Margibi (Mamba Kaba)	Deltamethrin	100	82.20%
		Cypermethrin	220	78.30%
	Montserrado (Careysburg)	Deltamethrin	73	60.40%
August	Montserrado (Careysburg)	Deltamethrin	84	29.20%
	Margibi (Mamba Kaba)	Deltamethrin	160	29.40%
	Grand Bassa (District #1)	Deltamethrin	25	12%
Sept	Margibi (Mamba Kaba)	Bendiocarb	44	100%
	Montserrado (Careysburg)	Cypermethrin	100	53.00%
Oct	Bong (Kpaai & Kokoya)	Fenitrothion	143	93.50%
	Margibi (Mamba Kaba)	Fenitrothion	40	97.50%
Nov	Margibi (Mamba Kaba)	Pirimiphos-methyl	91	100%
	Bong (Jorkole)	Deltamethrin	68	58.80%
	Bong (Kpaai)	Deltamethrin	101	51.50%
	Bong (Kpaai)	Pirimiphos-methyl	81	100%

Greater than 98% mortality in tube bioassays indicates full susceptibility, 90-97% mortality indicates probable resistance, and less than 90% mortality indicates resistance to the insecticide being tested.

---

[6] Liberia End-of-Spray Round Report 2012

The 2013 IRS campaign began in March 2013. However, due to the increased costs of non-pyrethroid IRS, only five high malaria burden districts in Bong County were targeted for IRS, totaling about 40,000 structures. See the table below for a summary of IRS activities in Liberia to date.

Liberia IRS Activities, Counties and Insecticide Class

Year	Counties					Statistics	
	Montserrado	Margibi	Bong	Nimba	Grand Bassa	Number of structures sprayed (coverage rate)	Population protected (%)
2009	X	pyrethroid	X	X	pyrethroid	22,000	160,000 (4%)
2010	pyrethroid	pyrethroid	X	X	pyrethroid	48,000	160,000+
2011	carbamate	pyrethroid	carbamate	pyrethroid	pyrethroid	89,710 (96%)	834,671 (22%)
2012	carbamate	carbamate	pyrethroid	pyrethroid	pyrethroid	96,901 (98%)	869,707 (23%)
2013	X	X	organo-phosphate	X	X	42,708 (96%)	367,930 (10%)

Challenges, opportunities, and threats

Insecticide resistance and the rising cost of IRS operations due to insecticide resistance pose a significant challenge to future IRS efforts in Liberia. Where testing has been conducted, significant pyrethroid resistance has been found, necessitating either twice yearly spraying with a carbamate class insecticide or once yearly spraying with a long-lasting organophosphate. Both options significantly increase the cost of IRS, limiting the number of people that can be covered with the current budget. Therefore, after consultations within the PMI interagency team and discussions with the NMCP, the decision was made to suspend PMI-supported IRS in Liberia after the 2013 spray round, and resources will be shifted to support LLIN procurements, since even in areas of pyrethroid resistance, LLINs act as a physical barrier and the irritancy of pyrethroids on the nets may still reduce mosquito blood-feeding.

It had been hoped that expanded public-private partnerships in Liberia could help to support the country's IRS program; however, in 2012 only Arcelor Mittal Liberia contributed to the operational costs of spraying in their concession areas, protecting about 6,000 people.

Entomologic capacity in Liberia is limited. Four entomology technicians were trained in 2010 at Noguchi Memorial Institute for Medical Research in Accra, Ghana. Two trainees were from the NMCP and two were from the Liberian Institute of Biomedical Research (LIBR). Additionally, the LIBR insectary, needed for production of insecticide-susceptible malaria mosquitoes as a baseline against which to compare field mosquito populations for determining resistance ratios is not functioning. Steps are being taken to modify a shipping container for use as a mosquito insectary, to be situated next to the NMCP.

Plans and justification

PMI is ensuring that former IRS-targeted districts receive special attention to avoid a resurgence of malaria. Districts in the former IRS-targeted counties of Montserrado, Margibi, Grand Bassa, Bong, and Nimba were already included in a mass LLIN distribution campaign in December 2012. PMI will prioritize these districts for additional BCC to promote LLIN usage, IPTp, and prompt diagnosis and treatment of malaria. In addition, PMI will continue to monitor entomological indicators and epidemiological indicators in former IRS-targeted districts in order to detect any upsurges in malaria transmission. Epidemiological indicators will be collected via HMIS. PMI will also assist the NMCP in setting up a comprehensive mosquito surveillance program in collaboration with the U.S. Naval Medical Research Unit No. 3 (NAMRU-3) from Cairo, Egypt, which has been surveying mosquito populations at sentinel sites in Liberia since 2011.

Proposed activities with FY 2014 funding ($394,000)

- Increase entomology capacity by providing equipment, supplies, and mentoring for NMCP entomology technicians. PMI will provide mosquito surveillance equipment to the NMCP to enable them to scale-up mosquito density, behavior, and species identification activities. NMCP technicians will receive equipment and training on the use of WHO tube and CDC bottle bioassay tests to begin nationwide surveillance for mosquito resistance. PMI will also support a full-time entomologist to sit with the NMCP to help build capacity and support training of insectary technicians. ($300,000)

- Malaria surveillance. Increase timely reporting and use of malaria data from HMIS for epidemiologic monitoring and early detection of increases in the number of malaria cases, or the severity of cases, in districts where IRS has been withdrawn. ($70,000)

- Provide technical assistance for vector control activities. CDC staff will conduct two TA visits to assist with training and to monitor planning and implementation of vector control activities. Training will include use of WHO tube and CDC bottle assays for insecticide resistance monitoring and mosquito collection techniques. In addition, mosquito surveillance activities will be reviewed. ($24,000)

3. Malaria in Pregnancy

NMCP/PMI Objectives

More than 170,000 pregnancies occur each year in Liberia and all pregnant women are at risk of malaria infection and its consequences. The NMCP's strategic plan has the following objectives for controlling malaria in pregnancy:

- To increase access to prompt and effective treatment of malaria in pregnant women to at least 80%
- To increase the use of at least two doses of SP for IPTp among pregnant women to at least 80%
- To increase the use of ITNs among pregnant women to at least 80%

Progress during last 12 months

PMI contributed to the development and testing of pre-service training materials focused on prevention and treatment of malaria in pregnancy. These materials were finalized and distributed to pre-service training institutions nationwide.

There are a total of 3,727 gCHVs across the country, 1,587 of whom are within USAID focus counties. In 2010, a curriculum to train general community health volunteers (gCHVs) was developed and training manuals produced. The manuals were used to train 390 gCHVs and trained traditional midwives (TTMs) on danger signs of pregnancy, malaria in pregnancy, and referral to ANC services. In 2011 and in 2012, 432 and 289 gCHVs respectively were provided with comprehensive community health education materials that stress early ANC attendance and prevention of malaria in pregnancy. Nationwide radio campaigns and printed posters also provide messages on prevention of malaria in pregnancy.

PMI has supported performance-based financing initiatives to improve IPTp coverage (and other indicators) at 99 of 157 health facilities in Bong, Lofa, and Nimba Counties and 24 out of 33 facilities in Grand Cape Mount County. This is accomplished through sub-contracts to nongovernmental organizations in these counties. There are indications that the performance-based financing initiatives have translated to improved ANC attendance. IPTp-2 coverage among pregnant women residing in catchment areas around USAID-supported facilities in Bong in 2012 was 79%, up from 70% the previous year.

National HMIS data from 2012 reported that 63,287 women received the second IPTp dose as part of their antenatal care—approximately 42% of the estimated 150,000 pregnant women who attended ANC at least once. This number is likely a poor estimate of coverage because of systematic deficiencies in recording IPTp at health facilities, facility-switching by pregnant women (i.e., women do not go to the same facility for each of their ANC visits), and incomplete reporting from facilities and county health departments. Nevertheless, this HMIS-based estimate of IPTp-2 coverage in 2012 is only eight percentage points less than the 50% estimate obtained from the 2011 MIS.

Challenges, opportunities, and threats

When the 2009 and 2011 Liberia MIS data are compared, core indicators for malaria in pregnancy show limited progress. The proportion of pregnant women who slept under an ITN only increased from 33% to 39% between the two surveys. Fortunately, ITN use in 2011 was 77% among pregnant women living in households with at least one ITN, indicating that lack of ITN ownership is a significant barrier to ITN use among this high-risk group.

Likewise, the national estimate for IPTp-2 increased from 45% to 50% between the 2009 and 2011 MIS. The NMCP and Family Health Division are working to strengthen ANC delivery at health facilities and through outreach efforts. ANC attendance rates in Liberia are generally high, with 96% and 66% of pregnant women attending ANC at least once and at least four times, respectively (DHS 2007).

Recent completion of a national plan to implement continuous ITN distribution at ANC sites will help increase household ownership and use of ITNs among pregnant women, assuming LLINs are adequately stocked and appropriately distributed. The NMCP and partners are considering additional continuous distribution mechanisms since the potential number of ITNs distributed through ANC alone is inadequate to sustain 85% household ownership (see ITN section).

Stockouts of SP, late presentation at ANC facilities, facility-switching behavior, and health worker performance are considered the most important modifiable barriers to improving IPTp coverage nationwide. The MOHSW now includes SP in its list of tracer drugs for performance-based contracts to help avert stockouts in health facilities. These contracts provide bonuses to health facilities for reaching IPTp targets. The system therefore provides incentives to health facility staff to work closely with traditional birth attendants and community health workers to ensure women attend ANC clinics early and repeatedly.

PMI is helping the NMCP to address deficiencies in recording IPTp by revising and redistributing ANC ledgers. In 2011, USAID conducted an assessment to identify technical, behavioral, and organizational factors affecting routine health data to guide the design of interventions to improve performance, quality, and use of data. A major finding of the assessment was that there is limited capacity to perform data quality assurance and data analysis in the county health offices and health facilities.

PMI and the NMCP support TTM efforts to refer pregnant women to ANC clinics rather than supply IPTp at the community level to encourage early and repeated ANC attendance. However, for pregnant women residing more than five kilometers from ANC services, outreach efforts by certified midwives to deliver ANC services, including SP, have been effective at increasing IPTp-2 coverage. The Family Health Division promotes this effort to ensure pregnant women comply with routine ANC visits. All health facilities with ANC services remain the primary source of administration of at least two doses of SP for IPTp.

Plans and justification

PMI will continue to help support the following NMCP policies to control malaria in pregnancy (MIP):
- All health facilities in the country (public and private) should provide IPTp according to the national MIP guidelines;
- The drug of choice for IPTp will be SP (procured by the Liberian government);
- The supply chain and management system should be strengthened to ensure availability of SP at ANC delivery points;

- gCHVs and TTMs should encourage MIP interventions by identifying pregnant women at the community level and referring them for early and repeated ANC attendance;
- Certified midwives will conduct outreach efforts to deliver a package of ANC services, including IPTp, to pregnant women living beyond 5 km of routine ANC delivery points; and
- ITNs will be distributed to pregnant women at ANC delivery points.

PMI will also join other partners in reviewing the new WHO IPTp guidelines with the NMCP, and, should there be a policy change from providing two SP treatments to pregnant women to providing SP at every ANC visit, PMI will assist in updating training guidelines and other documentation accordingly.

USAID-assisted districts (Nimba, Lofa, and Bong) will receive low-dose folic acid for supplementation during pregnancy as part of their essential medicines package. The GOL will be responsible for low-dose folic acid for the rest of the country, along with SP. Any SP gaps will be covered by the Global Fund.

Proposed activities with FY 2014 funding ($787,000)

- <u>Pre-service monitoring and supervision for malaria in pregnancy</u>. Monitor and evaluate adherence to new curriculum and clinical standards at the practicum sites (health facilities) associated with six clinical training sites. Joint visits with the Liberian Board of Nursing and Midwifery will occur quarterly and involve monitoring and supervision of the training institutions implementing updated MIP curricula and standards. ($25,000)

- <u>Perform an assessment</u> of the policies and practices of the malaria in pregnancy program in Liberia. The assessment will include an evaluation of ANC outreach services, as well as an evaluation of the status of implementation of the revised WHO IPTp guidelines and the impact of the policy change on reporting. In addition, best practices will be identified in selected counties with particularly high IPTp-2 coverage. ($150,000)

- <u>Distribution of MIP commodities</u>—LLINs and SP—through ANC delivery points. These resources will be routed to the Ministry of Health through the expanded Fixed Amount Reimbursement Agreement (FARA) mechanism, a direct channel to the Liberian Government, including the National Malaria Control Program and Family Health Division. Activities and deliverables will be achieved through MOHSW performance-based contracts with NGOs. ($150,000)

- <u>Continued in-service training and supervision</u> of health care workers at ANC facilities and in the community through performance-based incentives. These resources will be routed to the MOHSW through the FARA for performance-based contracts with NGOs, which include in-service training and supervision to the over 1,000 health workers in their 123 health facilities. In addition, the FARA supports the MOHSW and

County Health and Social Welfare Teams to supervise at least 75% of all health facilities every quarter. ($450,000)

- Technical assistance from CDC-Atlanta to support the plan and implementation of the MIP assessment. ($12,000)

4. Case Management

Diagnosis

NMCP/PMI Objectives

The National Malaria Strategic Plan stresses parasitological diagnosis for all suspected malaria cases at both the facility and community level, targeting at least 80% of patients with uncomplicated malaria receiving early diagnosis. RDTs are used in all health facilities, with microscopy as the preferred method where available. In addition, the MOHSW promotes the use of RDTs by gCHVs as part of iCCM. The MOHSW's long-term strategy is to have RDTs used at the community and clinic levels and microscopy at health center and hospital levels.

Progress during last 12 months

The diagnostic capacity for malaria continues to show progress. Although the 2012 Annual Report of the Ministry of Health and Social Welfare was not available at the time this Malaria Operational Plan was developed, data collected from health facilities via HMIS were available for 2010-2012. The number of facilities reporting malaria cases increased over that time period from 513 to 581 to 626 out of 657 facilities. The number of cases clinically diagnosed fell over the same period from 506,283 to 392,847 while the number of microscopic examinations increased by a corresponding amount from 670,356 to 772,363. In 2012, only 22% of all reported malaria cases were clinically diagnosed.

In order to encourage testing prior to treatment and increase access to recommended malaria medications, the MOHSW has made RDTs and ACTs available to private sector health care facilities at no cost with the expectation that those facilities will report via HMIS. In addition, the MENTOR Initiative has supported a pilot project to engage the private sector medicine shops and pharmacies in sections of Montserrado County in diagnosis before treatment and use of ACTs. Results of the pilot should be available by July 2013.

With PMI support, the revised National Therapeutic Guidelines are now consistent with the National Malaria Strategic Plan for confirmatory diagnosis of all uncomplicated cases of malaria. All public health facilities in Liberia have been instructed by the MOHSW to ensure compliance with these guidelines for managing malaria cases. The integrated management of childhood illness (IMCI) protocol for use in the community has also been updated as of February 2012 to include use of a malaria diagnostic test in the evaluation of febrile children - particularly those less than five years old. The IMCI protocol for use in health facilities has also been updated. PMI has supported training of community health workers in the new protocol, and has supported the purchase and distribution of RDTs followed by supportive supervision.

PMI support has led to the development of a transitional plan that will ensure that the National Diagnostics Unit (NDU) of the MOHSW assumes major responsibilities for managing diagnostics in Liberia. PMI is finalizing the installation of laboratory equipment in selected laboratories earmarked by the NDU. PMI continues to procure reagents and other supplies for the National Public Health Reference Laboratory (NPHRL), which is overseen by the NDU, to improve laboratory services. A technical working group provides a forum for the coordination of diagnostics among partners. PMI also continues to support the NDU to develop its capacity for procurement planning and forecasting of diagnostics equipment and supplies.

Challenges, opportunities, and threats

The treatment of suspected cases of malaria continues to pose a challenge to malaria control. Although microscopy capacity has increased, there is still a limited pool of laboratory technicians. As of October 2012 there were 318 nationwide, meaning that there is less than 1 trained laboratory technician per health facility. The situation is compounded by high numbers of consultations at health facilities, significant turnover in staff, and the expiration during the past year of the contract of the partner who had been providing technical assistance. The new implementing partner is developing a work plan that will focus on training of trainers to support cascade training of new staff and refresher training and supervision of existing staff. The work plan will also focus on the development of external quality assurance standards and systems.

Maintaining a regular supply of RDTs at the community and facility level, in addition to commodities and equipment for microscopy, remains a challenge of the supply chain management and distribution systems. Updating the indicators by which progress on malaria diagnostics is measured is also needed. Currently, the malaria treatment indicator in the FARA with the MOH reflects the prior emphasis on treating all fever in children under five as suspected malaria. It is worded to reflect administration of ACTs within 24 hours of onset of fever and does not indicate whether a diagnostic test was administered. As the indicator is updated, the HMIS and registers will need revision, and staff will need training on the new tools.

Logbooks for community health workers were not distributed until February 2013; thus prior reports were combined with those of the facility with which individual health workers were affiliated. Moving forward, the logbooks should enable better record keeping of diagnostics at the community level. In addition, the NMCP will have to continue advocacy efforts to ensure that clinicians conform to treatment guidelines. This effort will require the cooperation of professional groups, including the Liberia Medical and Dental Council, the Liberia Nursing Association, and the Pharmacy Association of Liberia, along with other affiliates.

Gap analysis

Gap Analysis for RDTs, Liberia CY 2013-2015*

Calendar year	2013	2014	2015
Projected number of RDTs needed	2,713,683**	1,776,613	1,727,545
Requested in Global Fund R10 Phase 2	0	1,022,650	1,138,689
PMI	2,500,000	1,750,000	1,750,000
TOTAL ANNUAL RDT GAP (SURPLUS)	**213,683**	**(996,037)**	**(1,161,144)**

* Revised projections submitted by the NMCP to the Global Fund as part of the Phase 2 application April 30, 2013
** Includes a onetime, six-month buffer

As part of the Global Fund reapplication process, for which PMI and other partners provided technical assistance, the NMCP revised the assumptions used to quantify projected RDT needs. The estimated annual number of febrile episodes for children under five was changed from 2 to 3, the number of episodes for adolescents was changed from 2 to 1, and the number of episodes for pregnant women and adults were held at 2 and 1, respectively. Other factors taken into consideration were the number of episodes that a MOHSW-supported health facility would manage and its diagnostic capacity, as well as positivity rates. The public sector is expected to manage increased episodes of malaria each year and to improve its diagnostic capacity. The estimates also reflect expansion of the MOHSW-supported efforts with private clinics, pharmacies, and medicine stores.

Plans and justification

The NDU, established in 2010, seeks to develop an integrated national laboratory system. The NDU has the mandate to oversee and supervise all diagnostic activities in clinical laboratories in the country, including the NPHRL, which routinely conducts quality assurance for the accurate preparation of slides. The NDU supports the external quality assurance program of the NPHRL. PMI will provide support for laboratories, and in collaboration with the Global Fund, will work to strengthen the diagnostic capacity of the MOHSW. PMI also promotes enhanced collaboration and communication between the NDU, NPHRL and NMCP in developing strategies regarding placement of new microscopes to expand diagnostic capacity, integrated supportive supervision using the County Diagnostic Supervisors and development of policies and procedures for an external quality assurance system using the knowledge and experience gained by the NDU and NPHRL in piloting external quality assurance systems for HIV (RDTs) and tuberculosis (microscopy).

Proposed Activities with FY 2014 funding ($1,827,000)

- Procurement of RDTs. The total need for RDTs is based on service delivery requirements, including public sector facilities, community case management, and private sector facilities. As the status of the Global Fund application will not be known prior to submission of the MOP, to assure continuity of operations, PMI will include procurement of 1,750,000 RDTs for 2015. Should the Global Fund purchase be approved, PMI will revise its support levels to fill any remaining gap in RDTs or elsewhere (e.g., LLINs for the nationwide campaign). ($1,295,000)

- Procurement of laboratory supplies, including Giemsa stain and other reagents for health facilities and the NPHRL, which will further strengthen the conduct of external quality assurance for malaria diagnosis. ($70,000)

- Support to extend the LMIS to track laboratory diagnostic supplies/reagents. The LMIS software has the capacity to track these supplies; PMI support will be aimed at developing materials and training to use the LMIS for this purpose. ($100,000)

- Implementation and monitoring of a diagnostics QA/QC system. The NDU Strategic Plan provides for an integrated approach to diagnostics in Liberia in all health facilities that includes both RDTs and microscopy. Under the Strategic Plan, the NDU will be expected to assume a greater role in ensuring proper malaria diagnosis through increased mentoring of laboratory personnel and validation. As microscopy becomes more widely used to diagnose malaria and monitor care of severe cases at health centers and referral hospitals, PMI will support refresher training for laboratory technicians to upgrade skills in malaria diagnostics. Twenty staff will be trained as trainers (the County Diagnostic Supervisor in each of the 15 counties and five central-level staff). The trained trainers will be mentored to conduct cascade trainings in their respective counties. Non-PMI funding from USAID and the Global Fund will provide additional financial support for these activities and the Clinton Health Access Initiative will provide additional technical support. ($200,000)

- Capacity development and supportive supervision. The MOHSW has directed that all treated malaria cases be based on confirmatory diagnosis. To ensure compliance with this policy change, the NMCP and NDU will continue support to health facilities to develop diagnostic capacity for early and accurate diagnosis of malaria. PMI will support capacity development and quarterly supportive supervision for over 1,000 health workers in 123 health facilities in select counties. This activity is primarily targeted at clinical staff and includes adherence to test results, whether at the point of care or performed in a laboratory. Global Fund and other donors are supporting similar activities in other counties not targeted by USAID. ($150,000)

- CDC will provide technical assistance to the NMCP through one dedicated diagnostic visit to support further efforts of the NMCP to rationalize treatment guidelines and improve malaria diagnostics and to develop and implement quality assurance systems at all levels. ($12,000)

Treatment and Pharmaceutical Management

Treatment

NMCP/PMI Objectives

The first-line treatment for uncomplicated malaria in infants, adolescents, and adults is fixed-dose artesunate/amodiaquine (AS-AQ). For severe malaria, the preferred treatment has been intravenous quinine or intramuscular artemether, and a shift in policy is being made to parenteral artesunate, including for pre-referral treatment. Oral quinine is recommended for malaria in children weighing less than 5 kg and in pregnant women in their first trimester.

Access to treatment of malaria with ACTs has been limited primarily to public health facilities and an increasing number of private health facilities supported by the MOHSW. The NMCP is further trying to increase access to appropriate case management to 80% of the population by through iCCM of malaria and through pilot programs in private sector medicine stores and pharmacies.

Progress during last 12 months

The revised 2010-2015 Malaria Policy and Strategic Plan focuses on increasing access to prompt and effective treatment with ACTs to 80% of the population. In 2012, the HMIS reported administration of 1.5 million ACT treatments, which represents an estimated 78% of the 1.8 million malaria cases reported that were either clinically diagnosed or positive by microscopy or RDT. At the community level, gCHVs are adhering to the MOHSW guidance to treat only cases of malaria confirmed by RDT and to refer persistent febrile cases to community clinics and health facilities. The revised ratio of one gCHV per 500 people, down from one gCHV per 1,000 people, will contribute to sustained progress. The Community Health Services Division of the MOHSW has also assigned community services supervisors to monitor the gCHVs and ensure that data is accurately and completely recorded and transferred to the HMIS. As noted above, special registers have been created and distributed to report data from the gCHVs as a separate component of the data reported by the health facilities with which the gCHVs are affiliated. PMI is collaborating with the Global Fund to support implementation of IMCI and the iCCM program for appropriate diagnosis and prompt treatment of uncomplicated malaria and for referrals for severe malaria.

Challenges, opportunities, and threats

The Liberia Medicines and Health Products Regulatory Authority (LMHRA), established with support from PMI in 2010, has attempted to address the problem of drug quality. PMI has provided training for personnel of the quality control laboratory of the LMHRA and has procured equipment and supplies to ensure the continued function of the laboratory. The Global Fund also supported the renovation of the quality control laboratory and procured additional equipment. PMI has provided technical support to the LMHRA through training and mentoring, and is currently assisting the LMHRA in setting up a registry for manufacturers of pharmaceuticals that will serve as a repository for initiating the detection of counterfeit antimalarials being imported into Liberia. Additionally, in 2012 the LMHRA issued a ban on malaria mono-therapy in the country.

There is a significant price differential between parenteral artesunate and artemether. In order to continue to provide the required number of treatments for severe malaria that PMI has been asked to support in the past, only artemether and quinine will be procured through PMI support. Artesunate will be included in the Global Fund application.

Other challenges include supply chain management (detailed in the Pharmaceutical Management section), supervision capacity, and a revolving staff in facilities, which makes it difficult to determine gaps in training.

Gap analysis

Gap Analysis for ACTs, Liberia CY 2011-2015*

Calendar Year	2013	2014	2015
National Needs	2,732,664**	1,772,702	1,671,653
PMI	2,700,000	767,000***	1,117,000
Requested in Global Fund R10 Phase 2	316,015	836,280	1,591,909
ANNUAL ACT GAP (SURPLUS)	**(283,351)**	**169,422**	**(1,037,256)**

* Revised projections made by the NMCP for the Global Fund application for Phase 2
** Includes a onetime, six-month buffer
*** 350,000 doses were purchased by PMI from FY 2014 funds to avoid a shortfall in 2013 of pediatric ACTs

Plans and justification

PMI will continue to support the NMCP's efforts to expand access to malaria case management through iCCM and partnerships with private health care facilities. PMI will continue to provide technical assistance to NMCP efforts, in collaboration with the MENTOR Initiative and the Global Fund, to support a private sector initiative to increase access to ACTs at medicine stores and pharmacies. RDTs will be included in this initiative to discourage clinical diagnosis.

Proposed activities with FY 2014 funding ($2,323,500)

- Procure ACTs. As the status of the Global Fund application will not be known prior to submission of this Operational Plan, PMI will assure continuity of operations by procuring about 1.1 million ACT treatments for the public sector, community case management, and private sector facilities in 2015. Should the Global Fund purchase be approved, PMI will revise its support to fill any remaining gap in ACTs or other needs. The apparent deficit in 2014 will be restored from 2013 stocks if the Global Fund request is approved. ($1,173,500)

- <u>Procure parenteral artemether and quinine to treat severe malaria.</u> PMI will procure a mix of these treatments for severe malaria. Quantities for FY 2014 are not yet known, but in 2013 PMI procured 373,000 quinine 200mg tablets, 558,000 quinine 300mg tablets, 58,900 artemether 20mg ampoules, and 155,500 artemether 80mg ampoules. ($200,000)

- <u>Capacity development.</u> The MOHSW has adopted an integrated approach to community-level treatment of three major childhood illnesses (malaria, diarrhea, and acute respiratory infections), which complements IMCI at the facility level. PMI will continue support for IMCI and iCCM for appropriate and prompt treatment of uncomplicated malaria and for referrals for severe malaria. Specifically, PMI will support:

    o <u>At the facility level,</u> capacity development and supportive supervision of 100 facility-based health workers in prompt and appropriate treatment of malaria; ($300,000) and

    o <u>At the community level,</u> training, equipment, supplies, capacity development, and supportive supervision for 1,587 gCHVs at a ratio of one gCHV per 500 people. Supervision visits will be monthly from district supervisors and quarterly from the central/county level. PMI will also support refresher training and follow-up of trainers and underperforming gCHVs. PMI is co-funding these activities with other partners. A national training curriculum is used and medications, logbooks, and RDTs are provided. ($550,000)

- <u>Monitor antimalarial drug quality.</u> PMI will continue to support the LMHRA for quality control and quality assurance of antimalarials through training and procurement of supplies, reagents, and equipment (e.g., sonicators, ultraviolet lamps, and titrators). This activity is geared towards strengthening the QA/QC laboratory that has been set up by the LMHRA to continue testing of randomly selected antimalarials from the private sector to ensure that these drugs are efficacious and meet treatment standards. Six people are being trained at the QA/QC laboratory, and nine staff members are being trained at the LMHRA. ($100,000)

<u>Pharmaceutical Management</u>

NMCP/PMI Objectives

Under the leadership of the MOHSW and in collaboration with partners, including PMI, a ten-year Supply Chain Master Plan was developed in 2010. The Master Plan integrates all pharmaceutical logistics into a single system to ensure transparency and responsiveness. The Supply Chain Management Unit has been re-established and is responsible for all supply chain operations.

Progress during last 12 months

With PMI support, LMIS tools, including a stock balance requisition and reporting form, were introduced into the supply chain system to institutionalize inventory management of commodities nationwide. Over the past year, the LMIS tools were increasingly used by health facilities in all the counties. The Supply Chain Management Unit has recorded an increase in the reporting rate of consumption data coming from all health facilities in 7 of the 15 counties in the country. There has been a gradual increase in the geographic coverage of counties where all the health facilities are regularly reporting useful consumption data, particularly for ACTs, and this is expected to increase through FY 2014. Following a year of reporting, the Supply Chain Management Unit will begin using the recorded consumption data to inform forecasting and procurement planning of malaria commodities. The storage and distribution of malaria commodities was also strengthened at the National Drug Service (NDS). PMI provided technical assistance for the revision of standard operating procedures for pharmaceutical management, including inventory management, distribution scheduling and tracking, warehouse management, and stock monitoring at the central level and in the counties. Additionally, PMI collaborated with the Global Fund to strengthen information technology services, allowing the NDS to generate stock level reports.

Challenges, opportunities, and threats

The supply chain system remains a challenge to the effective implementation of the Essential Package of Health Services, the cornerstone of Liberia's ten-year National Health Plan. Central to this problem is the unreliability of data emanating from health facilities in all counties to adequately quantify and forecast malaria commodities, although progress is being made with the roll out of LMIS tools. Distribution of malaria commodities is also hampered by limited storage at the NDS, poor procurement planning, and the lack of reliable means of transportation. The 2012 SLICE report also showed that the supply chain system in Liberia does not have a sufficient system in place to identify, document, and report inventory movement and transactions. These problems continue to contribute to intermittent stockouts of ACTs, SP, and RDTs.

The board of the NDS was recently reorganized and a task force established with the charge to document the existing problems, obtain a reliable stock count, and recommend measures to improve the security and capability of the commodity control system. The recommendations of the task force established by the NDS board addressed the splintered storage and distribution pattern of malaria commodities. The technical assistance being provided to the NDS by PMI has increased to ensure that a cohesive and coordinated storage and distribution system is institutionalized. The recommendations of the task force outlined measures aimed at addressing these problems through continued technical support to the NDS. Findings from the Public Financial Management Risk Assessment Framework (PEMRAF) Stage-2 Risk Assessment conducted by USAID in 2012 also highlighted technical and managerial deficiencies plaguing the NDS. The NDS has acknowledged these deficiencies and has affirmed its support for technical assistance to mitigate the risks identified in the PEMRAF. Moreover, the management of the NDS has aligned its support for the establishment of a state-of-the art, central warehouse as a viable option to address the shortfalls of the current storage and distribution system. These actions will further enhance PMI efforts in reducing the level of vulnerability of malaria commodities at all levels.

Plans and justification

PMI has initiated a customized supply chain system in Montserrado County to provide the NMCP and the MOHSW with a practical supply chain model that forecasts, quantifies, procures, and distributes based on reliable and accurate data. PMI has also strengthened its support to assist the NDS with mitigating the risks to commodities stored at the NDS through the implementation of the recommendations cited in the PFMRAF risk assessment report. In 2014, PMI will continue to support the supply chain system at both the central and county levels. PMI will support the establishment of a central NDS warehouse and will continue to mentor health workers at the county and health facility levels to ensure reporting via the LMIS.

Proposed activities with FY 2014 funding ($1,100,000)

- <u>Strengthening of the central drug and laboratory supply chain system</u>, including strengthening logistics and information systems, supervision, and forecasting at the central level. Specifically, PMI will support data collection and analysis for adequate forecasting and quantification; assist in developing a community-based supply chain management system for the iCCM program; and strengthen national procurement planning for commodities, equipment and supplies. In addition, PMI will ensure that the LMIS supports the HMIS. ($875,000)

- <u>Support to the supply chain at the county level</u> in four counties (Montserrado, Lofa, Nimba, and Bong), complementing Global Fund support in the remaining 11 counties. At the county level, specific activities will include LMIS support, monthly review and analyses of data received from health facilities, review of supply chain performance, and forecasting for procurement planning. In addition, PMI will support quarterly review meetings with health facilities, supportive supervision, and the distribution of commodities. ($125,000)

- <u>Warehousing of commodities at the central level</u>. PMI will support the furnishing and equipping a new NDS warehouse. ($100,000)

5. Monitoring and Evaluation Plan

NMCP/PMI Objectives

Liberia's National Malaria Strategic Plan 2010-2015 calls for monitoring the progress toward program goals and evaluation of the impact and outcomes of planned interventions. Additionally, the plan calls for the implementation of evidence-based program management. The NMCP's M&E strategy uses facility- and population-based indicators consistent with global standards and is fully costed.

Progress during last 12 months

The main activity in the last 12 months has been the planning and implementation of the 2013 Demographic and Health Survey. The DHS has a malaria module but is not including biomarkers, anemia or parasitemia. It is powered to provide data at the county level. Data collection teams were in the field at the time of the MOP visit (April 2013) and are expected to end data collection in July 2013. Preliminary results will be available during the first six months of 2014. The DHS is in line with the 2011 MIS and the MIS planned for 2015.

The MOHSW has a fully integrated computerized Health Management Information System (HMIS) based on data collected manually from health facilities through the county health teams that serves all departments and programs, including malaria care and treatment and distribution of nets at ANC and institutional deliveries. Personnel at all levels have been trained and the system is operational nationwide. Private health care facilities that receive commodities and support from the government and provide malaria diagnostic services, medications, and case management are also expected to report. Approximately 195 private facilities treat and report on malaria. Special registers to record community-based data from the gCHVs were distributed early in 2013 that will allow tracking. Currently, data from gCHVs is aggregated into that of the health facility out of which they operate. The system generates several monthly, quarterly and annual reports; increasingly, the data is being analyzed, frequently with assistance from the CDC PMI resident advisor, to inform local planning and evaluation, such as the recent Global Fund quantifications and the morbidity analysis that contributed to selection of sites for IRS in 2013. However, there are still issues with the quality, timeliness, and completeness of the data, and the system is still primarily used for the creation of required reports and underutilized for surveillance, supportive supervision, monitoring and planning. PMI is providing support to strengthen the collection, reporting, and use of HMIS data.

Index of availability of ACTs on the day of the End-Use Verification visit, July 2012

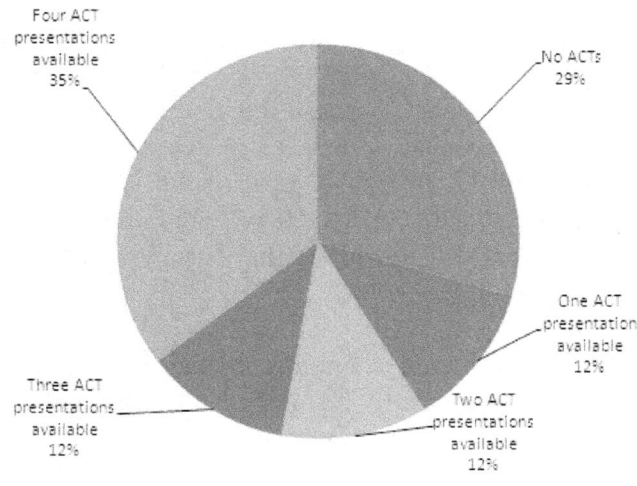

Source: USAID-SIAPS, PMI End-Use Verification, Liberia, July 2012.

In partnership with the NMCP and MOHSW Supply Chain Management Unit, PMI has supported seven End-Use Verification (EUV) surveys since 2010. The EUV is a rapid survey that collects data from 30-35 facilities each quarter on the availability of malaria commodities. The survey takes eight weeks from facility visits to the production of the final report, and includes a follow-up plan to correct any problems found. To date, a total of 395 health facilities have been visited—that is more than 50% of all health facilities in Liberia. Follow-up actions have included emergency procurements, training of health workers, and facilitating requisitions. EUV is implemented quarterly and provides information such as the graph above from the EUV conducted in July 2012 (last report available). Five (29%) out of 17 health facilities were stocked out of all four ACT presentations on the day of the visit. Only six (35%) facilities had all four ACT presentations required to treat all age groups.

There is currently a PMI-supported operational research study being conducted in Liberia. The study is field-testing the use of dried malaria-positive blood as quality control samples for malaria RDTs.

Challenges, opportunities, and threats

In spite of a sound M&E vision, the MOHSW and NMCP have had problems implementing their routine systems, such as the HMIS, because of limited technical capacity, funding, and oversight. HMIS managers report that most counties do not use data collected by their facilities for making local decisions. Additionally, the NMCP is severely short-handed in M&E and requires additional support in-house. There is only one person at the NMCP who is designated full-time to deal with all aspects of M&E, from policy setting to tool development to training and supervision.

Plans and justification

The NMCP M&E plan is integrated and financed by three sources, PMI, the Global Fund, and the Government of Liberia. PMI support to the NMCP's M&E strategy complements Global Fund support and will help provide key population-based indicators for monitoring malaria program implementation. PMI supports population-based surveys such as the DHS and MIS and provides technical assistance with the HMIS. PMI also supports data quality assurance and supportive supervision through the FARA with the MOHSW, while the Global Fund provides funding to support facility data, such as HMIS, health facility surveys, and supportive supervision for data quality assurance.

The Global Fund Round 10 Phase 1 grant included funding for therapeutic efficacy studies of the first-line malaria treatment. The NMCP is currently hiring consultants to conduct the studies by December 2013. PMI will support therapeutic efficacy monitoring in 2015.

Improving HMIS data reporting and use will be addressed jointly with the Global Fund and will focus on enhancing the NMCP's capacity to supervise and support counties and districts in their M&E activities. A CDC-supported evaluation of the HMIS system by an epidemic intelligence service officer took place in 2013 and should provide useful guidance on specific aspects of the system to target for improvement. The CDC PMI resident advisor is also mentoring the NMCP M&E lead on utilization of HMIS data to address specific questions, tailor supportive supervision to issues specific to each facility, and incorporate testing into the algorithm for treatment of fever in children under five.

The table below shows the main sources of data and sequence of surveys for malaria program monitoring and impact evaluations.

Data Sources for Monitoring and Evaluation in Liberia, 2005 – 2015

Data Source	Calendar (PMI) Year										
	2005	2006	2007	2008 (1)	2009 (2)	2010 (3)	2011 (4)	2012 (5)	2013 (6)	2014 (7)	2015 (8)
HMIS	X	X	X	X	X	X	X	X	X	X	X
Former sentinel sites	X	X	X	X	X	X					
DHS				X					X		
MIS			X		X		X				X
MICS											
Health Facility Survey	X				X				X		
Supervision and Evaluation Reports	X	X	X	X	X	X	X	X	X	X	X
End-Use Tool							X	X	X	X	X

Proposed activities with FY 2014 funding ($1,212,000)

- <u>PMI will provide resources to implement the End-Use Verification survey</u> on a quarterly basis. Emphasis will be placed on simplification of reports, dissemination of results, and follow-up action for any problems identified. ($80,000)

- <u>Strengthening data collection and dissemination for decision-making</u>. This is a follow-on activity that was included in the MOP FY 2013. The goal of the activity is to improve the collection, reporting, and use of HMIS data for decision-making at the district, county and national levels. Resources will be provided to support visits to health facilities by the NMCP to provide on-site support. ($50,000)

- Monitoring and evaluation support. A support person will be hired to sit at the NMCP to mentor existing M&E staff. S/he will build capacity for data QA and analysis. In addition, support will be provided for use of data generated by the HMIS and the LMIS, and to integrate that data with other information sources (e.g., health facility surveys). Mentoring of NMCP staff as they visit health facilities will also be provided. ($50,000)

- PMI impact evaluation. Liberia will be carrying out a DHS in 2013 and will have a second (follow-up) data point from the health facility survey to compare progress. The results of the DHS will be available in October/November of 2014. A PMI impact evaluation will be initiated shortly before the DHS results become available. ($120,000)

- Therapeutic efficacy monitoring. PMI will provide technical support and supplies for therapeutic efficacy monitoring at two sites. ($100,000)

- CDC will conduct one technical assistance visit to support the NMCP on monitoring and evaluation activities, particularly support for therapeutic efficacy monitoring. ($12,000)

- PMI will provide financial and technical resources to support the MIS in 2015. These resources are additional to those requested in FY 2013 and will complete full funding for the survey. The MIS will collect biomarkers (not collected in the DHS 2013). The sample size will be similar to the 2011 MIS, which sampled almost 4,500 households. This will be the fourth MIS. ($800,000)

6. Behavior Change and Communication (BCC)

NMCP/PMI Objectives

Liberia's National Malaria Strategic Plan 2010-2015 aims to target 90% of the population with malaria messages and 80% of civic groups, including community health committees, with advocacy activities through multimedia channels. Specific messages have been developed to address misconceptions, myths, and other barriers to appropriate malaria prevention and treatment. BCC outcomes will be measured through community surveys and/or population-based surveys.

Progress during last 12 months

Concerted efforts from PMI and the Global Fund, principal donors for BCC interventions in Liberia, have successfully raised the population's awareness of malaria. The 2011 MIS indicated that 97% of women of reproductive age have heard of malaria, of which 58% received messages from radio and 41% received messages from community health workers. The survey also showed that of women who have heard of malaria 65% reported that children are most affected, 27% mentioned that pregnant women are most likely to acquire malaria, and 82% cited mosquitos as the cause of malaria. Moreover, 92% of interviewed women said that there are ways to avoid malaria; 80% cited use of mosquito nets to avoid malaria. In addition, 97% of women know that malaria can be treated and 61% know to treat malaria with ACTs.

Malaria is part of the integrated service delivery package. During the past year, PMI, through its implementing partners, has assisted the MOHSW in developing communication materials and in training and equipping health promoters to convey malaria messages. PMI contributed substantially to bringing malaria information closer to communities through the activities of trained gCHVs. The integrated BCC campaign continued to promote the four priority interventions. As part of the mass media and social mobilization campaign strategy, PMI, in collaboration with the NMCP and the National Health Promotion Division, as well as other health partners, undertook the development of communication materials on early malaria case management, including posters and audio messages. The messages produced addressed prompt referral, early treatment, full compliance with treatment regimes, and home management for malaria.

Six hundred and sixty eight gCHVs, TTMs, and community health promoters have been trained to educate and engage communities on malaria using comprehensive community health education materials, which include information related to key malaria interventions. Partnerships were arranged with five community radio stations within Gbarpolu, Margibi, Cape Mount, and rural Montserrado Counties for the airing of pre-recorded ITN use radio spot messages (e.g., "Take Cover Under the Net"). In addition, with PMI funding, collaboration with the Ministry of Education to introduce malaria messaging in schools was initiated. Sample brochures targeting primary and secondary students have been developed and pretested and are being disseminated through various educational institutions as part of the early case management campaign.

A formative study has been initiated by the NMCP with support from the Global Fund to inform an update of the national communication strategy for malaria control. The study aims to identify behavioral determinants and misconceptions about malaria, to identify communication gaps associated with compliance with current BCC messages, and to generate evidence for new BCC interventions.

Challenges, opportunities, and threats

The 2011 MIS indicated high levels of knowledge of the population about malaria; however, it will take time to see this knowledge fully translated into desired behaviors or practices. In addition, given the MIS results showing that most people use nets when they are available, it is important to procure adequate supplies and commodities to the population when demands are created to support desired behavior changes. Radio and gCHVs have been shown to be the most frequent sources of information for the population; however, according to the last DHS, only 55% of the population possessed a radio. The NMCP has addressed this issue by advocating for more BCC activities through interpersonal communication. The coordination of BCC activities conducted by gCHVs and the supervision of the gCHVs by health facilities is a serious challenge because a number of different programs train and use gCHVs (e.g., the NMCP, EPI, National Aids Control Program, Family Health Division of the MOHSW, and National Tuberculosis Control Program). A mapping exercise of all gCHVs who have been trained and are operating in the country was conducted during 2012. The results of the exercise will assist the NMCP and its partners to better plan and follow up with BCC activities at the community level.

Plans and justification

To complement the Global Fund-NMCP formative study undertaken in 2012, the Health Communication Capacity Collaborative Project, implemented by the Johns Hopkins University Center for Communication, will conduct further research in 2013. The combined research will provide the foundation for the development of focused malaria messages to broaden the population's knowledge regarding malaria prevention and treatment. PMI will support the revision of BCC materials based on study results, as well as the development of tools for building interpersonal communication skills and the implementation of BCC activities.

The impact of PMI's contribution to behavior changes in Liberia will be measured through the monitoring of mass media and interpersonal communication interventions for malaria, and with the MIS planned in 2015.

Proposed activities with FY 2014 funding ($950,000)

- PMI will support the implementation of integrated interpersonal communication activities, including health care worker training, to promote all aspects of malaria interventions in Bong, Lofa, and Nimba Counties. Health workers who come in contact with mothers/caretakers regularly will be trained on how better to communicate preventive and curative messages, as health facility surveys have shown these skills to be poor. The Global Fund supports interpersonal communication activities in the other counties. PMI will support the training of health providers at the facility and community levels on developing interpersonal communications skills and community outreach capacities. ($350,000)

- Implementing and monitoring mass media malaria messages. PMI will support the NMCP in revising existing BCC materials and communication channels to provide focused malaria information to the population. In addition, PMI will support implementation of the revised national BCC strategy and the development of messaging for all malaria interventions, including the new WHO guidelines on IPTp and a focus on LLIN BCC. ($600,000)

7. Capacity Building and Health Systems Strengthening

NMCP/PMI Objectives

A high priority of the NMCP is to increase the qualifications of its staff, particularly in terms of their managerial and supervisory capacity. In addition, the Liberia MOHSW has made a commitment to integrate health services at both the health facility and the community level in order to improve access to health care.

Progress during last 12 months

The NMCP for the first time developed and disseminated the MIS 2011 report with minimum technical support from MACRO. The NMCP validated the iCCM manual that Plan International developed and provided technical supervision to Global Fund sub-recipients during training. PMI funds were used to conduct a preliminary capacity building assessment of the NMCP in 2012 using the WHO Six Building Blocks tool for systems strengthening. Priority areas identified for improvement include partner coordination and data management. Under the FARA, a reimbursement agreement with the MOHSW for health services delivery, the NMCP contributed to the production of the integrated MOHSW newsletter, which covers a range of malaria-related topics such as World Malaria Day events. The NMCP also participated in the integrated supportive supervision of health facilities.

PMI continues to work with other partners in health systems strengthening. PMI, in collaboration with the Global Fund, provided technical and financial assistance to the NMCP to develop the Global Fund Phase 2 proposal. Other collaborations with the NMCP and the Global Fund include coordination in supply chain activities and quantification of laboratory equipment and reagents, LLINs for routine and mass distribution, ACTs, and SP.

The NMCP has demonstrated leadership in revising and adapting its malaria policies to match international best practices. One example is transitioning its LLIN mass distribution strategy from rolling county-based campaigns to a more cost-efficient and technically effective single nationwide event. During the last year, PMI supported training on a modelling tool to help the NMCP assess the impact of various routine distribution routes and the number of LLINs that need to be distributed each year. In addition, the NMCP is working with PMI and WHO to incorporate new guidelines for IPTp during antenatal care.

Challenges, opportunities, and threats

The recent leadership change at the NMCP has created both a critical need and important opportunity to build managerial and technical capacity of key staff. Generally, Liberia continues to have a shortage of qualified health workers, and the provision of quality malaria-related services is still a major challenge. In addition, the country still lacks a well-functioning system to procure, distribute, and track malaria commodities (LLINs, ACTs, severe malaria kits, RDTs, etc.) in its 657 health facilities.

Plans and justification

PMI will continue its strong focus on building technical and managerial capacity for malaria prevention and control at all levels of the health care system. PMI will continue to support the NMCP to improve the quality, completeness, and timeliness of malaria-specific data reporting from health facilities and to increase staff skills in data analysis and interpretation. With the phasing out of its support for IRS, PMI will support the NMCP to strengthen its entomological monitoring capacity for potential future IRS interventions in Liberia.

The Malaria Steering Committee is an advisory body to the NMCP that is comprised of all malaria partners both local and international. The Steering Committee is tasked with providing technical and operational guidance for malaria control activities and with coordinating partners. However, recently its meetings have not been held regularly. PMI support will be focused on strengthening the Malaria Steering Committee by establishing technical sub-committees to allow more time and effort to focus on technical intervention areas.

Proposed activities with FY 2014 funding ($150,000)

Efforts will include strengthening the NMCP's capacity to conduct integrated post-training follow-up to health workers, providing technical support to strengthen NMCP managerial capacity, planning, supervision, and donor coordination, and improving linkages with the Family Health and Community Services Divisions of MOHSW. Technical assistance from PMI will complement Global Fund investments in NMCP capacity building. (Specific activities described in separate sections.)

- Support for the Malaria Steering Committee and its technical subcommittees. PMI will provide funding for the logistics of convening, documenting, and following up the actions of the Malaria Steering Committee and its technical sub-committees. Support will include meeting venues, transportation (if outside Monrovia), photocopying, and printing. ($20,000)

- Strengthening management, leadership and planning capacity of the NMCP. PMI will support technical assistance to strengthen the NMCP's management and oversight capacity via the Malaria Steering Committee and its technical sub-committees, both internally (e.g., meeting efficiency and setting timelines) and externally (e.g., donor and implementing partner coordination). With clear terms of reference and procedures for tracking its decisions and follow-up actions, the committee and sub-committees will provide more uniform technical guidance. ($130,000)

8. Staffing and Administration

Three health professionals, two serving as resident advisors (one representing CDC and one representing USAID) and a Foreign Service National, oversee PMI activities in Liberia. All PMI staff members are part of a single inter-agency team led by the USAID Mission Director. The PMI team shares responsibility for development and implementation of PMI strategies and work plans, coordination with national authorities, managing collaborating agencies, and supervising day-to-day activities. Candidates for resident advisor positions (whether initial hires or replacements) will be evaluated and/or interviewed jointly by USAID and CDC, and both agencies will be involved in hiring decisions, with the final decision made by the individual hiring agency.

The PMI professional staff works together to oversee all technical and administrative aspects of PMI, including finalizing details of project design, implementing malaria prevention and treatment activities, monitoring and evaluation of outcomes and impact, and reporting of results. Both resident advisors and other PMI staff members report to the USAID Mission Director. CDC supervises the CDC staff person both technically and administratively. All technical activities are undertaken in close coordination with the MOHSW/NMCP and other national and international partners, including the WHO, UNICEF, the Global Fund, World Bank, and the private sector.

Locally-hired staff to support PMI activities either in Ministries or in USAID will be approved by the USAID Mission Director. Because of the need to adhere to specific country policies and USAID accounting regulations, any transfer of PMI funds directly to Ministries or other host government institutions will need to be approved by the USAID Mission Director.

Proposed activities with FY 2014 funding ($1,020,000)

- <u>In-country staffing and administration.</u> Coordination and staff salaries and benefits, office equipment and supplies, and routine expenses for PMI activities in Liberia.

Table 1
President's Malaria Initiative - Liberia
(FY 2014) Budget Breakdown by Partner

Partner	Activity	Budget ($)	%
CDC	Technical assistance to various parts of the malaria control program	$60,000	0.5%
Deliver TO7	Procurement of LLINs, ACTs, severe malaria drugs, RDTs, and laboratory supplies; support supply chain management	$5,393,150	45%
Macro	Support Malaria Indicator Survey	$800,000	6.5%
TBD	Technical assistance for LLIN distribution planning; Entomological monitoring and increased surveillance in former IRS districts; PMI Impact Evaluation; Therapeutic Efficacy Monitoring	$778,000	6.5%
MalariaCare	Implementation and Monitoring of Diagnostics QA/QC system	$200,000	1.5%
New Mechanism (new bilateral cooperative agreement; will be an integrated health mechanism)	Supervision of pre-service training for MIP; Monitoring and documenting implementation of MIP; Strengthening data collection and dissemination for decision making; M&E support at central level; Implementing and monitoring mass media malaria messages; Support and TA for the malaria steering committee and its technical subcommittees	$1,025,000	8.5%
MOH/FARA	Integrated BCC for malaria control; support for MIP, malaria diagnostics, iCCM, and training activities, distribution of LLINs	$2,523,850	21%
GFATM/MOH/ FARA	Support for warehousing commodities	$100,000	1%
PQM	Monitoring of antimalarial drug quality	$100,000	1%
CDC/USAID	In-country staffing and administration	$1,020,000	8.5%
Total		**$12,000,000**	**100 %**